GOOD LUCK, BAD LUCK

Written by Rita Schlachter
Illustrated by G. Brian Karas

Troll Associates

Library of Congress Cataloging in Publication Data

Schlachter, Rita.
    Good luck, bad luck.

    Summary: Rabbit learns that it's his carelessness
and not a witch that is responsible for his many
accidents.
    [1. Rabbits—Fiction. 2. Behavior—Fiction.
3. Accidents—Fiction] I. Karas, G. Brian, ill.
II. Title.
PZ7.S34647Go   1986   [E]   85-14069
ISBN 0-8167-0572-0 (lib. bdg.)
ISBN 0-8167-0573-9 (pbk.)

GOOD LUCK, BAD LUCK

There was a knock on Rabbit's
door.
"Who is it?" asked Rabbit.
"It's me," said Bear.

"How do I know it's you?" asked
Rabbit.
"Open the door and you'll see me
standing here," said Bear.

Slowly, Rabbit opened the door
just a crack.
"It is you," said Rabbit. "I had
to be sure."

"Who did you think it was?"
asked Bear.
"I thought it was the witch,"
said Rabbit.

8

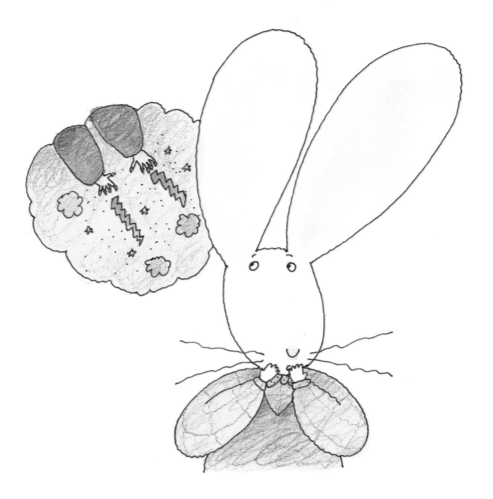

"Which witch?" asked Bear,
with a laugh. "Did one move
into the woods?"
"No," said Rabbit. "I'm talking
about the one who has cast a
spell on me."

9

Bear stepped inside and closed
the door. He heard something
rattle above his head. When he
looked up he saw a horseshoe
rocking back and forth.
"What's that for?" asked Bear.

"A horseshoe is good luck," said
Rabbit.
"Not if it falls on a friend's
head," said Bear.

"I'll fix it later," said Rabbit.
"But I need it in case the witch
comes back. Did you see her
broom outside by the front
door?"
"That's your broom," said Bear.

"Well, I know she was here,"
said Rabbit. "Maybe she's mad
because I forgot to set out milk
and cookies on Halloween."
"You set out milk and cookies for
Santa Claus on Christmas Eve,
not for the witch on Halloween,"
said Bear.

15

"That's good," said Rabbit.
"Then she can't be mad at me
for that."
"Why do you think the witch has
cast a spell on you?" asked Bear.

"Because of all the accidents,"
said Rabbit. "Yesterday when I
was running upstairs, the witch
pushed me and I fell."
"I always tell you not to run up
the steps," said Bear.

"That's not all," said Rabbit.
"When I was hopping to Squirrel's
house the witch pushed me into
a hole. I hurt my foot."
"You never watch where you're
going," said Bear.

18

"But I know the witch was here
while I was gone," said Rabbit,
"because when I came back the
front door was open."
"You never remember to close
it," said Bear.

Rabbit took an empty jar from
the cupboard.
"Will you help me catch a
spider?" he asked.

"Why do you want a spider?"
asked Bear.
"Spiders are good luck," said
Rabbit.
"You don't need a spider," said
Bear. "You just need to stop and
think before you do something."

But Rabbit didn't wait to hear
what Bear said. He was already
hopping down the road. He
hopped and hopped until he
came to a field of wildflowers.

"This looks like a good place to
find a lucky spider," said Rabbit.
"I don't think so," said Bear.

24

Rabbit didn't listen.
"*Mmmm*," said Rabbit. "The
flowers smell so sweet."
He danced around on one foot,
then he danced around on the
other foot. He picked a wild-
flower and put it to his nose.

"Ooooh!" said Rabbit. He threw the flower down. He started waving his paws back and forth in front of his face so fast you couldn't see them.

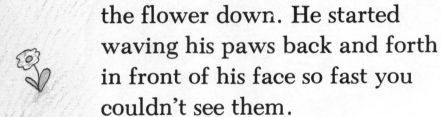

"Help! Help!" called Rabbit.
"It's a bee. Get him away."
"Just stand still," said Bear.

But Rabbit didn't listen. He kept
waving his paws and shaking his
ears. He hopped from side to
side. Then Rabbit hopped backwards. He hopped backwards
again and again and again.

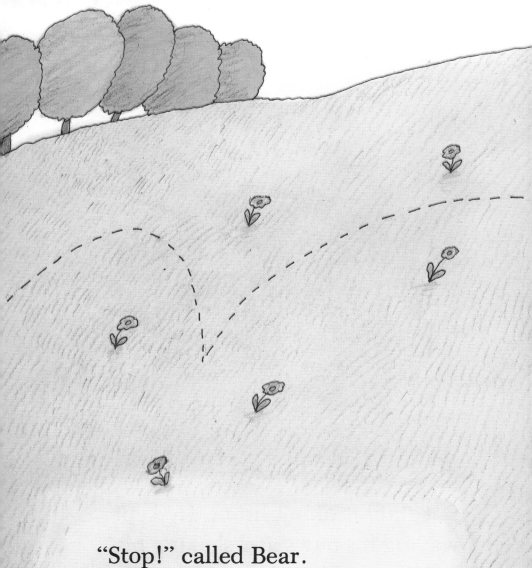

"Stop!" called Bear.
But Rabbit didn't hear him. He
hopped one more time and
landed right in the lake.

30

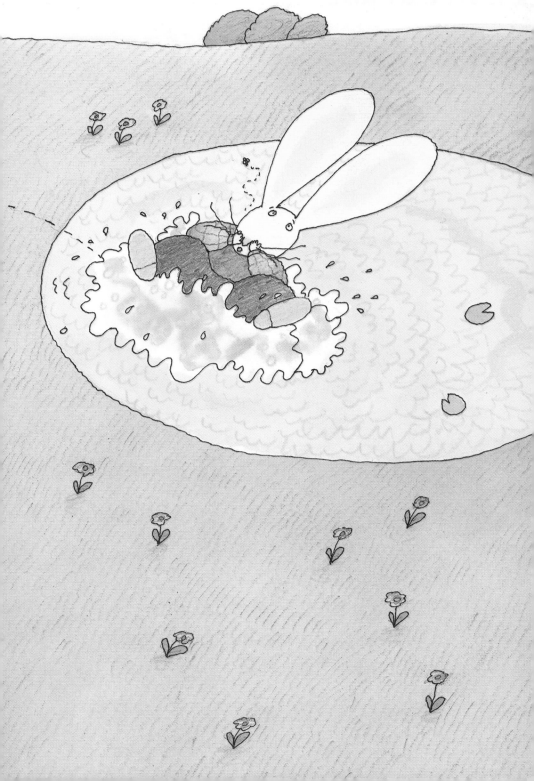

"Did you see her?" asked Rabbit,
wringing out his ears.
"See who?" asked Bear.
"The witch," said Rabbit.
"Didn't you see her push me into
the lake?"

"You fell into the lake because
you didn't watch where you
were going," said Bear.
"Why, you don't believe the
witch cast a spell on me, do
you?" said Rabbit.
"No," said Bear.

Rabbit twitched his nose, picked
up the empty jar, and hopped
on. He wasn't going to stop
looking until he found a spider.
He knew the witch was after
him, even if Bear didn't believe
it.

Rabbit looked under rocks, he
looked in an old hollow log, he
looked in the strawberry patch,
but there was no spider.

Rabbit knew the witch was watching him and sooner or later she would strike again. Then he looked up. Dangling right above his little pink nose was a spider!

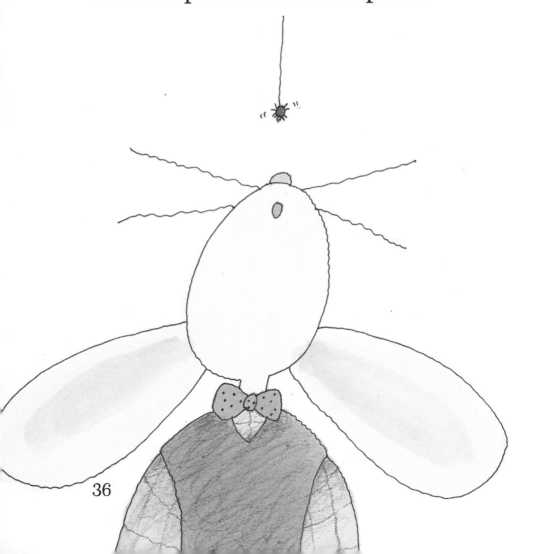

"Oooh! There's my lucky
spider," said Rabbit. "But I can't
reach him."
"That's the way he wants it,"
said Bear.

"Hurry! Hurry! Put him in the
jar," said Rabbit, jumping up
and down. "You can reach him."
"Okay, I'll help you," said Bear.
"But how can a spider trapped in
a jar bring you good luck?"
"I don't know," said Rabbit.
"But he will."

Rabbit hopped off, holding the
jar tightly between his paws. He
hopped slowly. He didn't hop
too high. He watched where he
was going.

40

"I made it!" said Rabbit.
"Nothing happened all the way
home. I told you the spider
would help me."
"It wasn't the spider," said Bear.
"You were just being careful."

Bear and Rabbit went inside. Rabbit closed the door hard. BANG! The horseshoe rocked back and forth. Then it fell on Rabbit's head. He dropped the jar. Quickly, the spider ran out across the floor, up the wall, and out the window.

"Your lucky horseshoe just hit you on the head and made you lose your lucky spider, who didn't save you from getting hit on the head with your lucky horseshoe," said Bear, all in one breath.

"You don't think there was a
witch, do you?" said Rabbit.
"You think all the accidents
happened because I didn't watch
what I was doing."

Rabbit thought for a minute.
"Maybe you're right," he said.
Then he picked up the horseshoe
and threw it outside. It sailed
through the air until it hit the
tree next door.

Mrs. Robin shook on her nest.
Squirrel lost his balance and fell
on Turtle, who was sleeping
under some strawberry leaves.

"I forgot to watch what I was
doing, didn't I?" asked Rabbit.
"You'll learn," said Bear, with a
smile. "You'll learn."

48